# My College Planner

Assess, Assemble, Afford, Achieve:
The only organizer made for college applications

# My College Planner

Assess, Assemble, Afford, Achieve:
The only organizer made for college applications

Honora Wall, M. A., Applied Curriculum and Instruction

PolyMath Publishing, Ocala, Florida

ISBN 978-0-692-06595-2
www.mycollegeplanner.org

# Table of Contents

# Introduction: College planning basics

## Applying for college

Congratulations! Deciding whether or not to go to college is an important decision. Now that you've decided that college is the right path for you, you will need to apply. It's an easy process, even though it feels overwhelming. Here are all the steps required to apply for college:

1. Decide that you want to go to college
2. Make a list of schools you want to attend
3. Gather personal information for the applications
4. Fill out paperwork online
5. Pay the application fee (if any, unless you have a waiver, based on need)
6. Wait for a response

That's it. Many people make the process more stressful than this, because they believe that "getting into the right school" will make or break their entire future. The truth is that your future will be decided by your work ethic and the opportunities you take advantage of. If you have a good grade point average (GPA), decent test scores (SAT or ACT), and an idea of what you want to study (your major), then you will find more opportunities available to you. If you don't have these things, you might find fewer opportunities and you might have to work harder to open more doors. Either way, there is no magical college or university that will make or break your career.

Whatever your background or current situation is, you can find the right college for you. This organizer will help you choose schools that are a good fit for you, gather the information you'll need, and plan the process so that your applications are turned in early and without stress (well, with less stress, at least!). The organizer was developed after more than a decade of working with high school students and adults who decided to apply for college. The methods in this book were tested and proven by the success of those students. You can trust that this organizer will help you, the same way it has helped hundreds of other students in your same situation.

## High school timeline

*A very generic guide, applicable for most students. For a personalized plan, visit www.mycollegeplanner.org*

**9th Grade:** College seems so far away! In some ways, it is. Most students have no need to think about college at this stage, unless you're interested in a military or Ivy League school. If you are, then Freshman year is the time to plan: look into the specific colleges you're dreaming of and find out what kinds of classes, GPA, and test scores they're looking for. For other students, make sure you keep that GPA as high as you can and get started on your community service hours. If you're thinking about a military academy or an Ivy League school, get the requirements now.

**10th Grade:** What are your interests? What types of jobs are available to people in the field you're interested in? How are your grades? Sophomore year is the time to analyze your possible goals and examine your weak areas. You'll take the PSAT this year, in preparation for the SAT and ACT tests. If you find that the PSAT is difficult, talk to a tutor or get a test prep book from your local library. You have time to prepare for great test scores; be sure to use the time wisely.

**11th Grade:** This is the year for students looking at competitive or specialty colleges: any school in the "Top 25" list for its field will have strict admissions guidelines. Find out what they are and align your GPA, test scores, and community service hours to them. Attend a pre-college summer program. For athletes, musicians, and performers, Junior year is the time to prepare for auditions, make promo reels of your performances and games, and make sure your GPA is solid. Start to fill in the tables in the index section of this workbook. Ask for letters of recommendations and work on your essays.

**12th Grade:** Most students start choosing a college this year. If that's you, you're not late to the game. The application deadlines could be as early as November or as late as May of your Senior year, depending on the school and whether you apply for early or regular decision. Early decision means that, if accepted, you promise to attend that school regardless of any other schools that might offer you admission. Early decision typically requires academic and talent standing above the recommended acceptance guidelines; most students apply for regular decision. This is the last year to take the SAT and ACT tests. You can have your scores sent to the college after you submit your application, but you will need to have your essay, resume, and community service complete.

The more competitive your first choice school is, the more time and energy you'll want to put into your high school transcript. Do you need to take AP classes? SAT Subject Area tests? Are there required math or science classes you need to take before you graduate? You might need to spend your summers taking classes online or through your local community college to make sure you have all the classes you need. If you are not planning to apply to a highly competitive college or university, you can take regular classes and maintain a high GPA. Either way, keep your college goals in mind as you go through high school.

> *"My College Planner is the perfect way to keep all of my important information organized-- passwords, deadlines, school requirements, and it is even has samples to guide you through this complicated process."* -- Simone, student

No matter where you're going or where you start from, there are some universal experiences to the college application process. First, you will be creating usernames and passwords and attaching e-mail accounts to numerous websites: College Board, ACT.org, the Common App, Coalition for College Access, SSAR, and more (we'll explain all that later). Use this chart to write down all the usernames and passwords for each website you use-- this step will save you hours of frustration! This chart comes first so that you can always find those usernames and passwords quickly.

**Websites, usernames, passwords**

| Website | Username | Password |
|---------|----------|----------|
|         |          |          |
|         |          |          |
|         |          |          |
|         |          |          |
|         |          |          |
|         |          |          |

## Organize your college plan

Just thinking about planning for college sends many students and families into a panic. How do you do it? What do you need to know? Are there any good tips out there? What if you pick the wrong school, miss a deadline, or can't get into the school you want? Are you starting too late?

Relax. This workbook will walk you through the process step by step. You will keep important papers, notes, and other ideas here. You can jot down tips, resources, and reminders, and have everything in one place for easy retrieval. Whether you're in 9th grade or 12th, or an adult going back to school, you can do this and you can do it yourself. This workbook will help you get where you want to go.

The workbook offers some advice and information, too. You'll read tips on finding the right college for you, getting an edge in your application, using your interests and skills to promote yourself, getting through the application process with minimal stress, and finding ways to pay for college. There are samples of a resume, an essay, and an email to college admissions representatives. Use the workbook to record your conversations with college advisors and keep track of important email addresses and phone numbers. During the college application process, you will speak with many people and receive lots of advice and opinions; keep all the information gathered in one place. This will make the application process easy and stress free.

Here are some tips to get you started:

**Tip #1:** Keep the workbook in a place where you can find it easily. You're going to create a record of websites, usernames, passwords, contact information, family information, and school transcripts. This information can be hard to compile at a moment's notice, and you don't want to lose it and have to start gathering everything again.

**Tip #2:** Add to the workbook over time. Don't try to write down everything in one day; questions, notes, resources, and options will develop over time. Also, don't expect to find the perfect school during your first search. Your perfect schools will come to you as you do more and more research. As you plan and organize, take your time and expect to go back to this workbook repeatedly. This way, you will reduce stress, aggravation, confusion. Also, going back to the workbook and calendar will keep you from missing any crucial deadlines.

**Tip #3:** Always have extra copies of important documents, and always store them in more than one place. I've worked with too many frazzled students who have lost their key papers or forgot to bring all of their documents to a college planning session. This wastes time and money, and increases stress. You can scan records (like immunization records) and email them to yourself. You can save letters of recommendation and essays both online and on your computer, and print copies to store in your workbook. Be sure to write down the usernames and passwords of your many websites here. You might also keep a list of them in your phone. Whatever you do, DO NOT rely on one copy, one place, or one means of storage. Always have extra copies of your documents.

**Homeschoolers:** *If you are a homeschooler, you may need to provide extra documentation or spend more time gathering school records and requesting paperwork. Many homeschool programs can generate an official transcript of your classes; contact your homeschool program provider for transcript requests. If you did not use an outside education program, your SAT and ACT test scores and a fantastic essay should be enough for your application. Give yourself more time to research the requirements that your college choices have for homeschool students. Homeschool students who are interested in more competitive colleges may want to take some of the SAT Subject Area Tests, in addition to the SAT, to show mastery in certain subject areas (check your preferred colleges first and see what they request). Visit www.mycollegeplanner.org for current information.*

---

**Adults returning to college:** *Older students applying for college will need copies of high school transcripts (and any previous colleges you may have attended). Even if you graduated from high school years ago, you can still order your transcript from your high school. Allow yourself extra time to track down phone numbers, reach school officials, and get your records. Have an official copy sent to the college you are applying to, and an unofficial transcript sent to you for your files. Many of our older clients fear stepping back into the classroom, but there's no reason to be nervous. Attending college is easier than you think! Don't be intimidated by the process.*

---

# Let's play Bingo!

*College Planning Bingo, that is.*

COLLEGE PLANNING BINGO™
*How many boxes can you claim?*

| GPA | EXTRA-CURRICULARS | TEST SCORES | CLUBS | COMMUNITY SERVICE |
|---|---|---|---|---|
| 2.0 or above | Paid Jobs | SAT: <900 ACT: <18 | 0-1 club | 5 or more hours (5-7 per year) |
| 2.5 or above | Community Organizations | SAT: 900-1200 ACT: 18-23 | 2-3 clubs OR >5 clubs | 30 or more hours (7-12 per year) |
| 3.0 or above | Sports Teams | **Community College Free Space** | Consistent clubs over time | 50 or more hours (12-18 per year) |
| 3.5 or above | Competitive Sports or Clubs | SAT: 1200-1400 ACT: 23-29 | Leadership positions | 75 or more hours (18-25 per year) |
| 4.0+ | Awards or Scholarships | SAT: >1400 ACT: >30 | Clubs that match major/minor | >100 hours (25 per year) |

The College Planning Bingo game is easy: the more boxes you have covered, the more schools you are a great fit for! Just remember, you can also find a great school, no matter how few boxes you have covered.

0-5 boxes covered: A quick search found between 50 and 75 colleges and universities across the country that would be a good fit for you. Additionally, community colleges are a great place to start your college career. You will save a lot of money and have a great college foundation that will allow you to transfer to more competitive colleges later.

6-10 boxes covered: You've already jumped up to over 600 colleges and universities that you would be a great fit for! Nice work, considering all it took was handing in homework on time, maybe taking a grade recovery class, or spending some time preparing for the ACT/SAT.

11-15 boxes covered: Nice work. You've added 500 more colleges to your growing list of choices! That's over 1100 schools for you to think about. You can easily choose between your preferred location, cost, and majors.

16-20 boxes covered: You should include some highly competitive schools in your search. There are literally thousands of colleges and universities that you will be a good fit for. Enjoy this nice reward for your hard work throughout high school.

21-25 boxes covered: Welcome to Ivy League level! Are you guaranteed a spot? No, not at all, but you're in the running, so apply. You can feel comfortable with your resume, scores, and chances of acceptance at almost any school. Your long-term dedication to your goals really shows!

| Your score: | Your plan to change it: |
|---|---|
|  |  |

# Chapter 1: Picking a college

*Making sense of an overwhelming amount of options*

What makes a college or university right for you? Is it the size, the location, the reputation? Or is it the total cost, the housing, the majors available to study? The bottom line is that the right college for you is the place where you will feel comfortable, welcome, challenged, and excited, and where you will learn new things without crippling yourself with a staggering student loan debt. Attending the best college for you can be a great springboard for your future. On the other hand, attending the best college for your friends or family, but not for you, can lead to a loss of years and money that you can't get back. Picking the right college is an important decision worthy of your time, attention, and research. Use this College Comparison Chart to help you find the right fit.

For more than a decade, students have said that the College Comparison Chart is the most helpful feature in this workbook. The columns are open for you to fill in your choices of schools. These will change over time, so use a pencil! Do you really have to write down the schools you're interested in? Yes! Having the options listed side by side helps students see the positives and negatives in a new light. This will make it easier to see which schools are a great match for you and will help you decide which schools you really want to apply to. The first column is filled out for you, as an example of what to include. Of course, school entrance requirements change regularly, so you should research the most recent information on the college website.

Pros/Cons/Other information: This space is for you to personalize your wants and needs. Are you close enough to commute? This could save you thousands of dollars in living costs. Would you like to be close enough to bring your dirty laundry home, but far enough away to avoid drop-in visitors? Do you want to explore a new climate, city, or state? Are you going for a four-year degree and then stopping, or are you setting yourself up for graduate school? Do you want a strong Greek community so you can join a fraternity or sorority? Note these considerations on your college comparison chart.

School Comparison Chart

| School | FSU (Example) | | |
|---|---|---|---|
| Location | Tallahassee/ urban/ woodsy | | |
| App Deadline | Nov 1 (early) or Feb 2 (regular) | | |
| App Fee | $30 ($200 admission deposit) | | |
| SAT | 1240 | | |
| ACT | 27 (21 minimum; 22 reading) | | |
| GPA | 4.0 (3.2/25/1800) | | |
| Major(s) | English Language and Literature; Psychology; Criminal Justice/Safety Studies; Finance; and International Relations and Affairs | | |
| Annual Cost | +/- $20,000 per year | | |
| Essay | Yes | | |
| Letters of Rec. | No | | |
| % Admitted | 46% | | |
| Pros/Cons/ Other Info | Dance, music, theater. SSAR; Coalition | | |

| | | | |
|---|---|---|---|
| School | | | |
| Location | | | |
| App Deadline | | | |
| App Fee | | | |
| SAT | | | |
| ACT | | | |
| GPA | | | |
| Major(s) | | | |
| Annual Cost | | | |
| Essay | | | |
| Letters of Rec. | | | |
| % Admitted | | | |
| Pros/Cons/ Other Info | | | |

| | | | |
|---|---|---|---|
| School | | | |
| Location | | | |
| App Deadline | | | |
| App Fee | | | |
| SAT | | | |
| ACT | | | |
| GPA | | | |
| Major(s) | | | |
| Annual Cost | | | |
| Essay | | | |
| Letters of Rec. | | | |
| % Admitted | | | |
| Pros/Cons/ Other Info | | | |

| | | | |
|---|---|---|---|
| School | | | |
| Location | | | |
| App Deadline | | | |
| App Fee | | | |
| SAT | | | |
| ACT | | | |
| GPA | | | |
| Major(s) | | | |
| Annual Cost | | | |
| Essay | | | |
| Letters of Rec. | | | |
| % Admitted | | | |
| Pros/Cons/ Other Info | | | |

## Location

Are you more comfortable on a large campus with plenty of room to explore and wander? Do you prefer a small campus that is easily manageable so you don't feel lost? Do you prefer an urban campus in a busy city, or would you enjoy living in the rolling countryside? How do you feel about extreme heat or cold? Would you like to stay close to home, or experience living somewhere far away? Location is an important factor in choosing a college that should not be overlooked. Visit, or take virtual tours, of different types of colleges and universities in different cities and states. In your first year, you will most likely live in a dorm and a car will not be allowed. Can you walk the campus easily? How big are the dorms? Will you have enough money to come home for the holidays and the summer break? How about the next three years? Are the nearby neighborhoods affordable and safe? Will you need a car? Are there jobs available in the area? Keep these questions in mind when you compare school locations.

*How do you pick a location? Rank your answers from 1 (disagree) to 5 (agree).*

| | | | | | | |
|---|---|---|---|---|---|---|
| 1. | I feel comfortable in new situations | 1 | 2 | 3 | 4 | 5 |
| 2. | I feel comfortable in familiar surroundings | 1 | 2 | 3 | 4 | 5 |
| 3. | I like to explore new areas | 1 | 2 | 3 | 4 | 5 |
| 4. | I like to stick with what I know | 1 | 2 | 3 | 4 | 5 |
| 5. | I enjoy meeting new people | 1 | 2 | 3 | 4 | 5 |
| 6. | I have a close circle of friends | 1 | 2 | 3 | 4 | 5 |
| 7. | I find my way around new places easily | 1 | 2 | 3 | 4 | 5 |
| 8. | I like to go to places I already know | 1 | 2 | 3 | 4 | 5 |
| 9. | I enjoy adventures and rarely plan my day | 1 | 2 | 3 | 4 | 5 |
| 10. | I like to be home for holidays | 1 | 2 | 3 | 4 | 5 |

Total from #'s 1, 3, 5, 7, 9: _____

Total from #'s 2, 4, 6, 8, 10: _____

If you have higher scores for the even numbered questions, larger schools are probably a good fit for you. If you chose higher scores for the odd numbered questions, then a medium or small campus might make you feel more comfortable. Remember, no quiz on paper can ever match an actual visit. Go to some colleges in your area and get a feel for what a college campus is like. Then you'll have a realistic opinion to base a choice on.

## Touring your top 3

If you can visit your favorite college choices, do! Seeing a campus and talking to students is a great way to know whether or not you should apply. Be sure to walk through the bookstore, the cafeteria, and the library. Ask about the class size, access to professors, and the dorms. You can register for a free tour with the school, or walk around campus on your own to get a feel for the layout. If you cannot visit your favorite school in person, you can take a virtual tour online.

| Schools near me that I can visit | Schools I want to travel to visit |
|---|---|
|  |  |
|  |  |
|  |  |
| Schools I can tour virtually | Groups I can travel with (School, church, etc) |
|  |  |
|  |  |
|  |  |

# Chapter 2: What to study

*Find your passion and follow your passion*

What do you want to do with your life? This simple question sends most students into a panic. Luckily, you don't have to know the answer right now. You can apply to college without choosing any one particular path of study. In this case, you will apply as "Undecided" for your major. Choosing Undecided will not count against you or make you "look bad" to a college or university. It simply means you're not sure and you want to explore your options. Of course, if you have a solid idea of your interests and goals, then it makes sense for you to choose a specific major. Either way, choosing a major or a minor simply affects the amount of classes you will take in a certain subject.

## Majors

Declaring a major states a specific interest and affects some of your class selection; for instance, a Biology major will have certain required classes that an English major does not. However, you can take those required classes at any time and you can choose other classes that interest you. College is very different from high school-- you will have some required classes, of course, but you will be free to take any class you wish, regardless of your major. You can also change your major while you're in school.

"Undecided" is the most popular college major, with approximately 20% of applying Freshmen declaring "undecided" as their major. In the admissions game, 20% of all applicants is a lot of competition. Choosing a popular major like Business, Psychology, English, or Communications will also put your name in a very large pile of applicants, while choosing Engineering, Math, or Science might reduce your competition. Of course, the reverse might be true at a STEM-driven school like MIT. Doing some basic research on the colleges and universities you want to attend will help you understand what different schools are looking for in an applicant.

When you choose a major to study, this selection drives your required classes. You should choose something you enjoy because you'll be learning a lot about this topic. What if you get in to a school you love but decide you hate your major? You can always change it. You would contact your advisor (similar to a high school guidance counselor) and fill out a form of intent to pursue the new major. Changing your major can delay your graduation date because you might need to take more classes in that area of study, so be sure to speak with your advisor about your decision.

## Minors

The difference between a major and a minor is the number of credit hours taken in a certain subject. You do not have to choose a minor. It's simply a way of saying, "I really love studying X, but I also really like Y, so I'd like to focus on both." A minor is not required, but it can help you be prepared for graduate school or certain careers. For instance, maybe you want to study forensics, but you prefer working in a lab or testifying in court or analyzing data instead of being out in the field working at crime scenes. In that case, you might major in Forensic Science and minor in psychology or statistics. You might want to work in politics or as a diplomat; in this case, you might major in Political Science and minor in Japanese (or vice-versa). Or, you might choose a major and not have a minor. Also, you can add or drop a minor at any time in your college career.

Possible majors, minors, and careers:

Jot down some ideas of things you like to do and the careers they lead to.

1. _____

2. _____

3. _____

4. _____

5. _____

6. _____

7. _____

8. _____

9. _____

10. _____

Now let's combine your interests with possible schools.

| Area of interest | Possible schools |
|---|---|
|  | 1.<br><br>2.<br><br>3. |
|  | 1.<br><br>2.<br><br>3. |
|  | 1.<br><br>2.<br><br>3. |
|  | 1.<br><br>2.<br><br>3. |
|  | 1.<br><br>2.<br><br>3. |
|  | 1.<br><br>2.<br><br>3. |

# Chapter 3: Getting an edge

*Moving to the top of the application pile*

Many colleges and universities are highly competitive, with hundreds or thousands more applicants than they have available spaces for students. However, you can give yourself an edge during the application process. You get an edge by establishing a personal connection with the school, cultivating a special skill or interest, or by carefully planning your classes and tracking your GPA if you begin early enough. Perhaps the most important way to get an edge is through writing a great essay.

## The essay

Oh, the pressure to write the perfect essay. Students can stare at the given prompt for days or weeks, wondering what to say. Many students think their essay needs to be a gut-wrenching tale of extreme hardship or written in iambic pentameter in order to make an impression. Luckily, neither of those things are true at all! Your essay needs to tell the college a little about you, how you think, and what's important to you.

College application essays are extremely short, usually around 500 words or less. That's a decent sized paragraph, no more. The Common App and Coalition have prompts you can choose from, and some schools have prompts of their own. Usually, the prompt asks you to talk about an event in your past or talk about your hopes for the future. You will need to stick to the prompt, be quick and concise, and choose great words that convey your exact meaning. A couple of quick tips to remember: Do not go over the word limit. Do not stray away from the prompt. Do not write your essay quickly once and submit it. Edit, edit, and edit again.

Of course, you want to submit the best essay you can. However, don't submit the best essay that your college planning coach can, or that your parent can, or that your friend can. As an educator, I can tell immediately which part of an essay or a project was completed by the student, and I can pinpoint exactly where an adult stepped in to help. So can the readers working in the admissions department at your favorite school. While another set of eyes or a springboard for ideas is always helpful, the final essay needs to be truly yours.

How do you write the best essay you can? Edit, edit, edit. Set aside time to edit again after that. Your essay should show the school two things: first, that you can write well; and second, that you have a passion you can relate to the prompt. Ask a teacher, parent, relative, mentor, pastor, or professional to read your essay. Be open to their suggestions.

Research examples of great college essays, but don't look for a magic formula. Make sure you answer the prompt. This shows that you know how to follow directions, which is always appreciated. Remember, essay readers see literally thousands of essays. They can see an essay that was written from the heart, and those always shine.

*NOTE: This essay is reprinted with permission from the author. This essay was written by a student who was later accepted to FSU; do not plagiarize it! This sample is here to give you some ideas, not to be used as your own essay.*

Sample Essay

The development of human nature and society has always stemmed from learning. It provides the skills and levels of intellect needed in order to create and build. Education is far beyond a letter grade and a standardized test score; it is liberty and opportunity. Every day of our lives is spent learning, from birth to death. Education does not end when you leave high school or college or when you find a career. While we learn about the outside world and the treasures within it, we also learn about ourselves. I believe that learning will be the most important aspect of my time at FSU. The classes I will take, the friends I will meet, and the memories I will make will stay with me throughout my life.

Our perceptions, our thoughts, our feelings are all connected to what we've learned through our everyday experiences. Through the experiences in my life, I have learned that I am passionate about justice and human nature. In 2011, I became a part of the Criminal Justice Academy at Jupiter Community High. This academy has solidified my interest in behavioral psychology and has shown me how I can make a difference in people's lives. The various cases we have studied have also shown me that while laws apply to all people, people's actions are individual. This is what fascinates me about behavioral analysis. With learning comes understanding, and as we understand why criminals act the way they do, we can help them understand their actions and better understand themselves. It is important to me to be a part of this process and I believe that the programs provided at FSU will prepare me for the challenges of working in behavioral analysis.

An individual is composed of all that they have learned. We are shaped by our victories and our failures. The things we learn are the only things that can never be taken away from us. This is what makes learning the most defining part of human nature. Learning is constant, exponential growth that leads to understanding. As we understand more, we are able to improve our current selves and the world for future generations to come. For these reasons I feel learning will be the most important aspect of my time at Florida State University.

## Essay Ideas

What will you write about? You will choose an essay prompt, which will give you the topic for your essay. The essay prompts will come from a website like the Common App or Coalition for College Access, or from the school's individual application (see the glossary for an explanation of these terms). When you research the college you want to apply to, their website will say which application form they use. The prompts are updated annually so be sure to check for the most recent prompts. Use this space to brainstorm some ideas for essay prompts and the topics you might write about.

| Prompt | Topic Idea |
|---|---|
|  |  |
|  |  |
|  |  |
|  |  |

## Make a personal connection

Making a personal connection with representatives of the school can help you determine if you're applying to the best place for you. You can find a list of regional advisors on the college website. They can guide you through the maze of applying, getting financial aid, and transitioning from high school to college. Reach out to them with an e-mail, letter, or phone call. Attend college fairs and speak with college representatives there. If you know your preferred major, reach out to the head of that department. Whenever you tour a college or meet someone at a college fair, get the name and email address of your tour guide or the school representative. Follow up with an email (or better yet, a handwritten note) within a week. This will allow you to develop a relationship and ask questions throughout the application process. Let the college know that you believe their school is the best place for you, and that you want to start a dialogue to see if they agree.

### Sample E-Mail

Hello Ms. Perrino,

My name is Angelina Rosa. I am a Junior at Lincoln High School in Wichita, Kansas. I have been researching colleges and I am very interested in applying to the University of Miami. I plan to major in Marine Science and I feel UM would be the best place for me to study.

I know that you are the Regional Advisor for my area. Please let me know any upcoming dates when you will be in or near Wichita; I would love to meet you in person and ask you about the University of Miami! If you will not be in Wichita, I am available to speak with you by Skype, phone, or email.

I am excited to begin my Senior year of high school and I look forward to applying to the University of Miami. I hope to hear from you soon. Thank you for your time.

Sincerely,

Angelina Rosa

School officials to contact

| School, contact name, & email | Date of contact | Response |
| --- | --- | --- |
| | | |
| | | |
| | | |
| | | |
| | | |
| | | |

## **Test scores and GPA**

If you begin planning for college early enough, in your first or second year of high school, you can open more college options by maintaining a high GPA and taking rigorous courses during high school. These include AP or IB classes, math beyond Algebra 2, Physics, or dual enrollment classes at your local community college. Most states require a 2.0 GPA or better to graduate high school, and most colleges are looking for a 2.5 GPA or better. Large universities with many applicants may want a 3.0, and competitive schools will look for 3.5 or even better than a 4.0 (gained through AP, IB, and honors classes).

Your test scores will come from the SAT and ACT tests. These are national tests covering math and reading, with optional essay portions. Community colleges do not require these test scores; colleges and universities have their own minimum test scores. Higher test scores will open up more college choices, but there is a school for you, regardless of your test score. Your GPA comes from your transcript. Request an unofficial transcript from your school guidance office.

|  | Mine | College requirement | Plan to make them match |
|---|---|---|---|
| GPA |  |  |  |
| HPA (Honors GPA) |  |  |  |
| SAT Score |  |  |  |
| ACT Score |  |  |  |
| Other |  |  |  |

There are many ways to get your GPA or test scores to the level they need to be. Some resources are free, like tutoring through members of the National Honors Society at your school, YouTube videos (check out my channel, GetMathFast, for math help), or by getting books at the library. Some resources involve a fee, like private tutoring or taking test prep classes. Explore all your options. Visit www.mycollegeplanner.org for more ideas and resources.

Changing your grade point average can be as simple as turning in homework on time, every time. It can require taking a class for a second time over the summer in order to get a higher grade. It might involve taking Honors classes, which count for a higher grade point average than a regular class. A word of caution: don't take AP, AICE, IB, or other high-pressure classes just because you heard that you should. These classes typically require more reading, writing more papers, taking high-stress tests, and completing many hours of homework. If this pace isn't comfortable for you, you won't do well and your GPA will suffer. Most students get more bang for their buck if they prep for the SAT and ACT tests rather than take more advanced classes that can hurt their GPA.

Changing your test scores will require an intervention of some kind: tutoring, taking a test prep class, or exploring other resources. My favorite tip is to read the Answers & Explanations section in the back of a test prep book. This section explains what the test writers had in mind when they wrote the test, and it is invaluable information.

## Chapter 4: Skills and interests

*Making good use of the things you like to do*

Your skills and interests can lead you to your major. They can open up community service opportunities, offer resume building opportunities, and lead you to scholarship opportunities. They might even be a great topic for your essay. Not to mention, being involved in sports, clubs, and community groups helps you grow as a person and as a student. Write them down here and see where they take you.

## Extracurricular activities

Were you a varsity volleyball player in your freshman year? Have you been a competitive bowler since elementary school? Are you the volunteer who has logged the most hours at the local pet shelter? Did you organize a club at your high school? If you have a special skill or interest, let the college know. You might invest in a professional audition or highlight reel that you can send to a coach or the head of the drama department. You might create an online portfolio of your artwork or have a blog detailing your experiences as a volunteer in the community. Brainstorm all the things you've done, who the contact person or supervisor was, and look up their address and phone number. You will use this on your resume and in your application. Community service hours, volunteer opportunities, summer programs, and jobs all go here. Use this information to complete your resume, add to your application, and generate scholarship search ideas.

| Skill/ Interest | Supervisor/ Contact | Address/ Phone | Dates of involvement |
|---|---|---|---|
|  |  |  |  |
|  |  |  |  |
|  |  |  |  |
|  |  |  |  |

## Sports and clubs

If you play a sport, any sport at all, look for schools that have a strong program for your particular sport (even better is a school that wants to build a stronger program). This is especially true for golf, bowling, lacrosse, volleyball, and other sports which may not get television attention but can give you an edge in applying. You may qualify for a scholarship you hadn't even thought of; for instance, thousands of scholarship dollars are left on the table every year for golfers and bowlers who don't plan to continue their sport in college. This can be a big mistake. If your college has a club or team for your sport, and it probably does, you can continue to be involved in something you enjoy and you can meet people who will help you feel part of the school community. This is true for any of your interests, like chess, debate, theater, yearbook, gaming, or dance. No matter what level your level of involvement is, find a school that matches or challenges it.

| Activity | Dates Involved | Coach/Sponsor | Contact Information |
|----------|----------------|---------------|---------------------|
|          |                |               |                     |
|          |                |               |                     |
|          |                |               |                     |
|          |                |               |                     |

## Hobbies and other interests

Of course, there are many interests and hobbies that don't involve a club, organization, or competition. These are still valuable and worthy pursuits that can help you determine your career path and your right school. Avid readers, gamers, runners, knitters, movie watchers, and music lovers can all find success while doing what they enjoy. Look for schools that have clubs or classes that meet your interests. Research careers that involve your interests; you might find a surprising path you hadn't thought of which is perfect for you. Begin by listing your interests, then match them to classes, clubs, and careers.

My Hobbies and Interests

1. _____

2. _____

3. _____

4. _____

5. _____

## Chapter 5: Gathering information

*Write it down now and never have to search for it again*

In this section, we will cover the minimum items you should gather before you start your application. The vast majority of colleges and universities only accept online applications, meaning you can begin an application, save it, and return to complete the application at a later time. Writing down personal, family, and school information can save you time and frustration by having this information handy before you begin. Use the tables in the index section to store your social security number, birthdates for you and your parents, your home address, phone number, and current email addresses for you and your parents. You will need the address and phone number of your high school and any places where you have worked or volunteered. If you are applying to school as an in-state resident, you will need the dates each of your parents began living in that state. Many schools use either the Common Application or the Coalition website, both of which allow you to fill out one application form, write essays, and submit to the schools of your choice.

Family information

| Name and Birthdate | Address | Phone | Email |
|---|---|---|---|
|  |  |  |  |
|  |  |  |  |
|  |  |  |  |
|  |  |  |  |

## Letters of Recommendation

You can use a letter of recommendation for your college application, a summer internship or specialty program, or for a job interview, so be sure to ask for a copy you can keep. Check the college or university requirements to see if they require a letter of recommendation or not. Your letter cannot come from a family member; ask a pastor, teacher, coach, mentor, or other adult who knows you academically or personally.

Don't rely on one person to write a glowing letter; you might miss a deadline while you wait. Most people are happy to help, but are overwhelmed with other obligations. If you are hoping to get three letters of recommendation, ask six people. If you plan to ask a teacher or coach for a letter of recommendation, do it near the end of Junior year. Once Senior year begins, your entire class will be asking for letters of recommendation and teachers will not have time to write all of them. When you ask someone to write a letter for you, give them a copy of your resume. They will want to include specific information about your achievements. Whoever you ask, you will add their name and email to your college application and the person will send in the letter directly to the school.

Letters of Recommendation List

| Person to ask | Email Address | Date asked | Response | Resume Sent |
|---|---|---|---|---|
|  |  |  |  |  |
|  |  |  |  |  |
|  |  |  |  |  |
|  |  |  |  |  |
|  |  |  |  |  |

## Resume

It's never too early to start writing your resume. Having a resume that you can update as needed will save you time, frustration, and ensure that you don't forget important information or activities. You can easily add or update information at any time, but it can be difficult to remember all of your achievements, employment, and volunteer experiences when you create your resume for the first time (especially if it's the middle of senior year). Write down as much contact information as you can for everyplace you have worked or volunteered. Include clubs and sports team as well.

Your resume should include your personal information, school achievements, hobbies and clubs, employment history, and special skills. You should include up to three personal or professional references. These can be teachers, tutors, mentors, pastors, or other adults, but not family members. Keep your resume to one page unless you are applying for a specific program, like theater, where a longer resume is expected.

Resume information

| School/Jobs/ Organizations | Address/ Phone Number/ Dates Attended or Employed |
|---|---|
|  |  |
|  |  |
|  |  |
|  |  |
|  |  |
|  |  |

## Sample resume

**Josie Williams**
354 Fairway Drive North                                     **Cumulative GPA:** 3.4
Lake Worth, FL 33460
Cell: (555) 310-3737
josie.williams@nomail.com

**Education**
Jupiter Community High School, Criminal Justice Academy, Jupiter, FL. 2011-2015.
Anticipated graduation date May 2015.

**Volunteer Experience**
Interact Drama Camp, 2013. Counselor for children 4-16.
Beach Clean Up, 2013. Criminal Justice Academy.
Jupiter Homecoming Parade, 2012. Criminal Justice Academy. Traffic Control.
School Fair, 2012. Criminal Justice Academy.
Jupiter Jubilee, 2011 and 2012. Criminal Justice Academy.
Criminal Justice Annual Car Wash, 2011-2013.

**Clubs/Organizations**
Gay Straight Alliance Club, 2014-2015.
Debate Club, 2013-2015.
Fictional Literature Club, 2011-2012.

**Awards/Certifications**
National Catholic Forensic League Grand Nationals, Competitor, 2014.
PBCFL Grand Finals, Top 6 National Qualifier in Oral Interpretation, 2014.
Florida Forensic League State Finals, Semi-Finalist in Oral Interpretation, 2014.
Honor Roll, 2013-2014.
National Youth Leadership Forum on National Security: Exploring American Diplomacy, Intelligence, and Defense, Nominee, 2013.

**Hobbies**
Writing
Theater/Musical
Film
Debate

**Employment**
Wellington Country Club, June 2011-January 2012. Babysitter, Hostess, Busser. Responsibilities included observation of client's children, seating clients to tables, organizing reservations, assisting waiters and maintaining a clean and proper appearance of the club.

Art Shows, 2008-2013. Sales Associate. Responsibilities included setting up tents, maintaining care of artwork, assisting artists, and sales.

# Chapter 6: Paying for college

*How do I pay for this? Ah, there's the rub*

College can be very expensive. College can be very affordable. College can be free. The choice is yours because you pick your college path. No one should let fear of cost or debt stop them from attending college. Find unique ways to cut down on your out-of-pocket costs and be realistic about the amount of debt you want to take on. You could research scholarships frequently, utilize work-study programs, or start your college career at a community college to save money.

## The cost of college

The world is full of affordable schools offering a solid education. There are even schools that offer a quality degree for free, if you're willing to work, have a low family income, have an interest in living commune style, or have an interest in studying overseas. Community colleges offer 2-or 4-year degrees almost entirely covered by Pell Grants (government funding you don't pay back). Open your search to include these free and low cost options.

Carefully consider the long-term cost of student loans--the average student spends around 20 years paying off their Bachelor's Degree! This may be common, but it is not necessary. Use a combination of scholarships, work-study programs, jobs that help pay for college, loans, and careful choosing to keep the cost of college manageable. You may want to pursue an Associate's at a community college and get all of your core classes out of the way at a rate that might be covered by a Pell Grant or part-time job.

College can be very expensive if you attend a private school or go out-of-state. These costs will be paid for with student loans, Parent Plus loans, or private lender loans. Remember to consider the true cost of attending a school, above and beyond the tuition price. It's better to overestimate your total cost than it is to be surprised by a bill you didn't think of. Housing, food, books, travel, clothing, and entertainment will also cost you a pretty penny. The cost of travelling home for the holidays, important birthdays, or for the summer should be included. Some of these will be added into your loan amount (housing, a school-based meal plan, and books) while others are out-of-pocket (travel to and from school, clothing, etc.).

# College savings plan

*A brief chart of the money available for you to pay for college*

| Type of funds | Amount |
|---|---|
| Family or Personal Savings | |
| Pell Grant (if qualified by FAFSA) | |
| Federal Loans (if qualified by FAFSA) | |
| Private Loans | |
| Other Funds | |
| Total | |

## FAFSA

The FAFSA, Free Application for Federal Student Aid, is found at www.fafsa.gov. It is a free application that determines how much financial aid, if any, you qualify for. Family income will determine your expected family contribution (EFC) to pay for college, which affects the amount of aid you will be offered. This EFC is based off of your family tax returns, and your FAFSA information is sent to the schools you select. Your colleges will use the FAFSA and other information to create your financial aid package. If you are concerned with your ability to pay for college, talk to your college financial aid advisor. They will help you navigate the financial aid process and explain your many options. Simply applying for the FAFSA does not require you to take the offered loans, so you can feel comfortable about exploring your options without necessarily securing a loan.

## Grants, loans, and scholarships

After you fill out the FAFSA and get accepted to a college, the school will let FAFSA officials know the cost of tuition, housing, and other fees. If that amount is more than your grant award and financial aid award from the school, you will be asked to pay out-of-pocket or take out loans to cover the difference. There are many options for these loans, including student loans and Parent Plus loans from the government or loans from private lenders. Many times, you will be offered more than you need for tuition, and this can help pay for rent and food when you live off-campus. However, be careful not to take more than you need, or your loans can overwhelm your post-graduation salary.

Grants, unlike loans, are not paid back. Neither are scholarships. The Pell Grant will be offered by the FAFSA first, before any loans. After the Pell Grant, look for scholarships you might qualify for. Any scholarship money you can find will pay your tuition and fees and reduce the amount of loans you'll need. Consider all of your interests, hobbies, activities, and family history when you research scholarships. There are some unique ones out there, although they might be hard to find: if you bowl, play golf, are left-handed, or taller than 6'3", you can find a scholarship. If you are the first generation in your family to attend college, or have experienced exceptional hardship, or have volunteered a large number of hours or for many years at one place, you can find a scholarship. Other funds for college can come from local community service organizations, if you establish a connection with them while in high school. You might consider working for a company that helps pay tuition for its employees. Also, ask about work-study programs that can reduce the amount of your tuition. This is a great way to facilitate meeting new friends on campus and give you valuable work experience.

Use this chart to generate ideas for unique scholarships you may qualify for. List the website and deadline. The more you write down your ideas, the more ideas you will think of. When you write them down, you will remember them later when you have time to research scholarships. Write down the websites you visit so that you can go back to them later when you are ready to apply.

| Skill/Interest/Etc. | Applicable Scholarship | Deadline | Response |
|---|---|---|---|
|  |  |  |  |
|  |  |  |  |
|  |  |  |  |
|  |  |  |  |
|  |  |  |  |

# Final thoughts: Choose the right path

There are many different ways to reach your goals. You may leave home and spend four years at the college or university you always dreamed you would attend. You may find yourself transferring as your interests and experiences change. You may need an extra year (or a few years) before you are ready to commit to a college degree, or before you are able to pay for college. If you are determined to obtain a college degree, you will reach your goal, however long or by whatever means it takes. Be open to many ideas.

Starting your college career at a community college can be an inexpensive way to complete core classes, raise your GPA, and prepare to leave home. Most states offer programs where students can complete their Associate Degree, maintain a certain GPA, and be eligible to transfer to any state university. This can save you money and open new opportunities that might be closed to you right after high school graduation. It is also a good option for students who test poorly and have low SAT and ACT scores.

Preparation and organization are the key to making your college application process stress-free. Give yourself enough time to finish paperwork, applications, and essays before they are due. Organize your papers and ask for help when you need it. Use the Internet and the library to find all the information, guidance, and examples you need. Remember to give yourself plenty of time to relax with family and friends, too. These experiences are worth much more than any degree.

# Glossary

*Some 4-1-1 to get you started.*

## College vs. University

What's the difference between a college and a university? Here are some basics you should know: A college is an institute of higher learning that offers Associate's and Bachelor's degrees; a university also offers graduate degrees. Colleges and universities may be public or private institutions. Public colleges are funded by the state they operate in and are usually very large: large campus, large classes, and a large choice of majors and minors. Private colleges are funded by students, alumni, and donors. They usually have smaller campuses and class sizes, and they may have fewer majors to choose from, since private colleges will have a smaller area of focus. Many students choose between the two based on cost (public schools offer a reduced tuition rate for in-state students), size, or reputation in a certain career field. Either choice gives you a great education and preparation for life when you pick the right place for you.

Community colleges are non-profit schools that offer two or four year degrees and a variety of trade programs. Typically, the tuition rate is very reasonable and the schedule of classes is flexible. SAT and ACT scores are not required for admission. Students will take a placement exam that determines their level of math and reading classes. A degree from community college will allow you to apply to any four-year college or university without losing credits for classes you've taken. This is great option for any student who wants to save money on college education.

There are also a growing number of for-profit schools, with mostly online programs. For-profit colleges and universities offer accelerated degree tracks with high tuition rates. Caution: before you sign up for an online, for-profit school, do plenty of research! Be sure they have accreditation from a reputable group, that the tuition is reasonable, and that the graduation rate is high. Honestly, your local community college is probably a much better choice-- with much lower tuition costs.

## Reach vs Safety schools

A "reach" school is a college or university that you would love to attend, but you're not sure if you have the test scores and grades to get in. A "safety" school is one you feel very confident of being accepted to. Every student will have their own definition of "reach" and "safety". While some people recommend that you apply to a reach school, a safety school, a state school, and a group of schools "within range", there is no magic number of applications you should send or schools you should apply to.

## Common App vs. Coalition for College Access

These are both online application portals that are used by hundreds of colleges and universities. They can cut down on time and aggravation, since you only have to enter your information once and it can be submitted to many schools. They are free to use, although you will pay an application fee to the schools you apply to.

## SSAR vs Transcripts

The SSAR (Student Self-reported Academic Record) is a free website portal that allows you to input all of your high school level classes, in every subject. Some colleges like to see a SSAR and some will take your transcript without also having you fill out the SSAR. Check with the schools you are applying to. Your transcript is an official record of all the classes you have taken throughout your school career. You will request your transcript from your school's guidance office; an unofficial transcript is useful for your records, while an official transcript has to be sent from the guidance office to the college directly.

## GAP vs HPA (aka Unweighted vs Weighted GPA)

GPA stands for Grade Point Average, on a 4.0 scale. An A on your report card equals 4 points, a B is 3 points, C is 2 points, and a D is 1 point. Your grade points are added together and divided by how many classes you've taken. An F is worth zero points, which can really drag down your average: the points you have are divided by a larger number of classes, making your GPA lower. The GPA is usually an unweighted score, which means all classes count for the same points, regardless of how easy or difficult the class is considered to be. HPA stands for Honors Points Average, which means a difficult class counts for more points. Your HPA is usually higher than your GPA, and can be higher than a 4.0 score.

Use the calendar on the next page to fill in important dates: application deadlines, SAT and ACT tests dates, and class tests and projects. Write in when you will work on your essay and when you will study. Include vacations and holidays so that you have planned breaks. Write down college fairs and tours. Most of your college application work will happen between October and March of your Senior year.

## JULY

| Sunday | Monday | Tuesday | Wednesday | Thursday | Friday | Saturday |
|--------|--------|---------|-----------|----------|--------|----------|
|        |        |         |           |          |        |          |
|        |        |         |           |          |        |          |
|        |        |         |           |          |        |          |
|        |        |         |           |          |        |          |

# AUGUST

| Sunday | Monday | Tuesday | Wednesday | Thursday | Friday | Saturday |
|--------|--------|---------|-----------|----------|--------|----------|
|        |        |         |           |          |        |          |
|        |        |         |           |          |        |          |
|        |        |         |           |          |        |          |
|        |        |         |           |          |        |          |

# SEPTEMBER

| Sunday | Monday | Tuesday | Wednesday | Thursday | Friday | Saturday |
|--------|--------|---------|-----------|----------|--------|----------|
|        |        |         |           |          |        |          |
|        |        |         |           |          |        |          |
|        |        |         |           |          |        |          |
|        |        |         |           |          |        |          |

# OCTOBER

| Sunday | Monday | Tuesday | Wednesday | Thursday | Friday | Saturday |
|--------|--------|---------|-----------|----------|--------|----------|
|        |        |         |           |          |        |          |
|        |        |         |           |          |        |          |
|        |        |         |           |          |        |          |
|        |        |         |           |          |        |          |

# NOVEMBER

| Sunday | Monday | Tuesday | Wednesday | Thursday | Friday | Saturday |
|--------|--------|---------|-----------|----------|--------|----------|
|        |        |         |           |          |        |          |
|        |        |         |           |          |        |          |
|        |        |         |           |          |        |          |
|        |        |         |           |          |        |          |

## DECEMBER

| Sunday | Monday | Tuesday | Wednesday | Thursday | Friday | Saturday |
|--------|--------|---------|-----------|----------|--------|----------|
|        |        |         |           |          |        |          |
|        |        |         |           |          |        |          |
|        |        |         |           |          |        |          |
|        |        |         |           |          |        |          |

# JANUARY

| Sunday | Monday | Tuesday | Wednesday | Thursday | Friday | Saturday |
|--------|--------|---------|-----------|----------|--------|----------|
|        |        |         |           |          |        |          |
|        |        |         |           |          |        |          |
|        |        |         |           |          |        |          |
|        |        |         |           |          |        |          |

# FEBRUARY

| Sunday | Monday | Tuesday | Wednesday | Thursday | Friday | Saturday |
|---|---|---|---|---|---|---|
|  |  |  |  |  |  |  |
|  |  |  |  |  |  |  |
|  |  |  |  |  |  |  |
|  |  |  |  |  |  |  |

# MARCH

| Sunday | Monday | Tuesday | Wednesday | Thursday | Friday | Saturday |
|--------|--------|---------|-----------|----------|--------|----------|
|        |        |         |           |          |        |          |
|        |        |         |           |          |        |          |
|        |        |         |           |          |        |          |
|        |        |         |           |          |        |          |

APRIL

| Sunday | Monday | Tuesday | Wednesday | Thursday | Friday | Saturday |
|--------|--------|---------|-----------|----------|--------|----------|
|        |        |         |           |          |        |          |
|        |        |         |           |          |        |          |
|        |        |         |           |          |        |          |
|        |        |         |           |          |        |          |

# MAY

| Sunday | Monday | Tuesday | Wednesday | Thursday | Friday | Saturday |
|--------|--------|---------|-----------|----------|--------|----------|
|        |        |         |           |          |        |          |
|        |        |         |           |          |        |          |
|        |        |         |           |          |        |          |
|        |        |         |           |          |        |          |

*"My College Planner helped me stay organized and gave me important information and tips, all in one place!" -- Cassidy, student*

Made in the USA
Middletown, DE
28 February 2020